A Father's Book
of Wisdom

Compiled by H. Jackson Brown, Jr.

Rutledge Hill Press
Nashville, Tennessee

Published in Nashville, Tennessee, by Rutledge Hill Press, Inc., 513 Third Avenue South, Nashville, Tennessee 37210.

Typography by BesType, Nashville, Tennessee.

Library of Congress Cataloging-in-Publication Data

A Father's book of wisdom / compiled by Jack Brown.
   p. cm.
  ISBN 1-55853-018-5
  1. Quotations, English. I. Brown, Jack, 1940-
PN6081.F33 1989
082—dc19   89-3517
                                         CIP

Printed in the United States of America

9 10 11 12 13 14 / 94 93 92

A few weeks after Dad passed away, we found eight shoeboxes in his closet. They were filled with scraps of paper, old envelopes, napkins, matchbook covers, little blue spiral notebooks – even cash register receipts – all covered with ideas Dad thought were profound, interesting, or merely amusing. Obviously, Dad had grabbed whatever paper was available whenever he had felt inspired.

Some of the notes were quotations from books and articles he had read, but many were original insights and observations.

Dad had always been a reader, a thinker, a kitchen-table philosopher. We were thrilled to discover this rich legacy of his intellect, wit, and wisdom.

We sorted through all the writings and compiled this book. It's a book about one father's view of life and what he thought about the importance of self-reliance, commitment, love, generosity and success.

We hope you'll enjoy reading it. Dad never told us how to be successful and happy – he just gave us the opportunity to watch him do it.

Table of Contents

Other books by H. Jackson Brown, Jr.

Life's Little Instruction Book
P.S. I Love You

Don't let what you cannot do interfere with what you can do.

— *John Wooden*

Pride makes us do things well. But it is love that makes us do them to perfection.

— *Dad*

Winning is not a sometime thing; it's an all-time thing. You don't win once in a while, you don't do things right once in a while, you do them right all the time. Winning is a habit. Unfortunately, so is losing.

— *Vince Lombardi*

The harder you work, the luckier you get.

— *Gary Player*

Behold the turtle. He makes progress only when he sticks his neck out.

— *James B. Conant*

The secret is to become wise before you get old.

— *Dad*

First you forget names, then you forget faces, then you forget to pull your zipper up, then you forget to pull your zipper down.

— Leo Rosenburg

When you were born, you cried and the world rejoiced. Live your life in such a manner that when you die the world cries and you rejoice.

— *Old Indian saying*

When an old person dies, a library is lost.

— *Tommy Swann*

Nothing is good or bad, but thinking makes it so.

— *Shakespeare*

To travel hopefully is better than to arrive.

— Sir James Jeans

Two stonecutters were asked what they were doing. The first said, "I'm cutting this stone into blocks." The second replied, "I'm on a team that's building a cathedral."

— Old Story

Regardless of what company you work for, never forget the most important product you're selling is yourself.

— Dad

When you dance with your customer, let him lead.

— *Dad*

Challenges can be stepping stones or stumbling blocks. It's just a matter of how you view them.

— Unknown

I am only one; but still I am one. I cannot do everything, but still I can do something; I will not refuse to do the something I can do.

— *Helen Keller*

In matters of style, swim with the current; in matters of principle, stand like a rock.

— *Thomas Jefferson*

When the One Great Scorer comes to write against your name, He marks, not that you won or lost, but how you played the game.

— *Grantland Rice*

If you don't stand for something, you'll fall for anything.

— *Unknown*

Hold yourself responsible for a higher standard than anyone else expects of you. Never excuse yourself.

— Henry Ward Beecher

If you were to sell your character, would you get full retail, or would it go for a bargain-basement price?

— Dad

You never know a man's character until you've shared a bowl of peeled shrimp with him.

— Dad

Courage is resistance to fear, mastery of fear, not absence of fear.

— *Mark Twain*

Don't be afraid to take big steps. You can't cross a chasm in two small jumps.

— David Lloyd George

What matters is not the size of the dog in the fight,
but the size of the fight in the dog.

— Coach Bear Bryant

One man with courage is a majority.

— *Andrew Jackson*

If you judge people, you have no time to love them.

— *Mother Teresa*

When you judge others, you are revealing your own fears and prejudices.

— *Dad*

I will speak ill of no man, and speak all the good I know of everybody.

— *Ben Franklin*

Let the refining and improving of your own life keep you so busy that you have little time to criticize others.

— Dad

Praise in public. Criticize in private.

— *Dad*

We're constantly striving for success, fame and comfort when all we really need to be happy is someone or some thing to be enthusiastic about.

— Dad

A group of two hundred executives were asked what makes a person successful. Eighty percent listed enthusiasm as the most important quality.

— *Source Unknown*

Excellence is never an accident.

— *Dad*

Oh, the difference between nearly right and exactly right.

— *Dad*

The quality of a person's life is in direct proportion to their commitment to excellence, regardless of their chosen field of endeavor.

— *Vince Lombardi*

It's a funny thing about life; if you refuse to accept anything but the best, you very often get it.

— *Somerset Maugham*

Well done is better than well said.

— *Ben Franklin*

I t's not how far you fall, but how high you bounce.

— Dad

Some goals are so worthy, it's glorious even to fail.

— *Unknown*

If your life is free of failures, you're not taking enough risks.

— *Dad*

Don't judge those who try and fail. Judge only those who fail to try.

— *Dad*

When you have been wronged, a poor memory is your best response.

— *Dad*

Don't carry a grudge. While you're carrying the grudge the other's guy's out dancing.

— *Buddy Hackett*

Forgive and forget. Sour grapes make for a lousy wine.

— Dad

Do not use a hatchet to remove a fly from your friend's forehead.

— *Chinese Proverb*

A friend is a gift you give yourself.

— *Robert Louis Stevenson*

To have a friend, be a friend.

— *Old Saying*

Happiness is not an absence of problems; but the ability to deal with them.

— *Dad*

Most people are about as happy as they make up their minds to be.

— *Abraham Lincoln*

Success is getting what you want. Happiness is liking what you get.

— *Dad*

To be without some of the things you want is an indispensable part of happiness.

— *Bertrand Russell*

Happiness is an inside job.

— Dad

Prefer a loss to a dishonest gain; the one brings pain at the moment, the other for all time.

— *Chilton*

Dishonesty is like a boomerang. About the time you think all is well, it hits you in the back of the head.

— *Dad*

No legacy is so rich as honesty.

— *William Shakespeare*

When you tell the truth, you never have to worry about your lousy memory.

— *Dad*

Honesty is the first chapter in the book of wisdom.

— *Thomas Jefferson*

M an's mind once stretched by a new idea, never regains its original dimension.

— *Oliver Wendell Holmes*

You see things that are and say, "Why?"
But I dream things that never were and
say, "Why not?"

— *George Bernard Shaw*

Imagination is more important than knowledge.

— *Albert Einstein*

$\mathbf{A}$lways be a little kinder than necessary.

— James M. Barrie

There are no unimportant jobs,
no unimportant people,
no unimportant acts of kindness.

— Dad

There is no experience better for the heart than reaching down and lifting people up.

— *John Andrew Holmer*

I expect to pass through life but once. If, therefore, there be any kindness I can show, or any good thing I can do to any fellow being, let me do it now, for I shall not pass this way again.

— *William Penn*

This is the final test of a gentleman: his respect for those who can be of no possible value to him.

— *William Lyon Phelps*

The smallest act of kindness is worth more than the grandest intention.

— Dad

$\mathbf{R}$eal generosity is doing something nice for someone who'll never find it out.

— Frank A. Clark

Never let a day go by without giving at least three people a compliment.

— *Dad*

We don't know one millionth of one percent about anything.

— *Thomas Edison*

All that mankind has ever learned is nothing more than a single grain of sand on a beach that reaches to infinity.

— Dad

The manager administers, the leader innovates.
The manager maintains, the leader develops.
The manager relies on systems, the leader relies
on people. The manager counts on controls, the
leader counts on trust. The manager does things
right, the leader does the right thing.

— *Fortune Magazine*

Love doesn't sit there like a stone, it has to be made, like bread; remade all the time, made new.

— *Ursula K. Le Guin*

Treasure the love you receive above all. It will survive long after your gold and good health have vanished.

— *Og Mandino*

Who, being loved, is poor?

— *Oscar Wilde*

You will find as you look back upon your life
that the moments when you have really lived
are the moments when you have done things
in the spirit of love.

— *Henry Drummond*

Men always want to be a woman's first love; women have a more subtle instinct: what they like is to be a man's last romance.

— *Unknown*

For an instant, love can transform the world.

— Dad

We two form a multitude.
— *Ovid*

Marriage is an empty box. It remains empty unless you put in more than you take out.

— *Dad*

B y all means marry; if you get a good wife, you'll become happy; if you get a bad one, you'll become a philosopher.

— Socrates

If you're looking for a big opportunity, seek out a big problem.

— Dad

A wise man will make more opportunities than he finds.

— *Francis Bacon*

P roblems are opportunities in work clothes.

— *Henry Kaiser*

In the middle of difficulty lies opportunity.

— *Albert Einstein*

There is no future in any job. The future lies in the man who holds the job.

— *George Crane*

Don't wait for your ship to come in. Row out to meet it.

— Dad

There is only one pretty child in the world, and every mother has it.

— *Chinese Proverb*

Fathers are pals nowadays because they don't have the guts to be fathers.

— Dad

When I was a boy of fourteen, my father was so ignorant I could hardly stand to have the old man around. But when I got to be twenty-one, I was astonished at how much he had learned in seven years.

— *Mark Twain*

Train up a child in the way he should go, and when he is old, he will not depart from it.

— Proverbs 22:6

A father is a banker provided by nature.

— *French Proverb*

In the game of life even the 50-yard line seats don't interest me. I came to play!

— *Dad*

Do it! Move it! Make it happen! No one ever sat their way to success.

— Dad

Nothing in the world can take the place of persistence. Talent will not; nothing is more common than unsuccessful men with talent. Genius will not; unrewarded genius is almost a proverb. Education will not; the world is full of educated failures. Persistence and determination alone are omnipotent.

— *Calvin Coolidge*

Success seems to be largely a matter of hanging on after others have let go.

— *William Feather*

In the confrontation between the stream and the rock, the stream always wins – not through strength but by perseverance.

— Dad

The man who wins may have been counted out several times, but he didn't hear the referee.

— H. E. Jansen

Never, never, never, never give up.

— *Winston Churchill*

We do not see things as they are. We see things as we are.

— *Dad*

Our thoughts determine our responses to life. We are not victims of the world. To the extent that we control our thoughts, we control the world.

— *Dad*

What you see is what you get – except in pre-packaged strawberries.

— *Dad*

The display of status symbols is usually a result of low self-esteem. The self-confident person can afford to project a modest image.

— Dad

No one can make you feel inferior without your consent.

— *Eleanor Roosevelt*

Always consider yourself a first-class citizen of the world. No one deserves better treatment than you.

— Dad

Be good to yourself. Be patient. Be kind. Be forgiving. After all, you're all you've got.

— *Dad*

The closest we ever come to perfection is when we write our résumés.

— Dad

Send someone a telegram that reads "Congratulations." Regardless of who he is, he'll think he's done something the past week to deserve it.

— Dad

When an archer misses the mark, he turns and looks for the fault within himself. Failure to hit the bulls-eye is never the fault of the target. To improve your aim – improve yourself.

— Gilbert Arland

Self-reliance is the greatest gift a parent
can give a child.

— Dad

Self-reliance is like a flashlight; no matter how dark it gets, it will help you find your way.

— Dad

You are free the moment you do not look outside yourself for someone to solve your problems.

— *Dad*

Not in time, place, or circumstance, but in the man lies success.

— *Charles Rouce*

He has achieved success who has lived well, laughed often and loved much.

— *Bessie Anderson Stanley*

Any failure will tell you success is nothing but luck.

— *Dad*

Failure is success if we learn from it.

— *Malcomb S. Forbes*

Success is best measured by how far you've come
with the talents you've been given.

— *Dad*

The road to success is not doing one thing 100 percent better, but doing 100 things one percent better.

— *Dad*

Behind every successful man stands a proud wife and surprised mother-in-law.

— Brooks Hays

Success comes before work only in the dictionary.

— *Anonymous*

We make a living by what we get, but we make a life by what we give.

— *Norman MacEwan*

The true measure of success is not what you have,
but what you can do without.

— *Dad*

There is never a wrong time to do the right thing.

— Dad

I'd rather have roses on my table than diamonds on my neck.

— *Emma Goldman*

It's not hard to make decisions when you know
what your values are.

— *Roy Disney*

I'd like to be rich enough so I could throw soap away after the letters are worn off.

— *Andy Rooney*

I'm opposed to millionaires, but it would be dangerous to offer me the position.

— *Mark Twain*

Wealthy people miss one of life's great thrills –
making the last car payment.

— Dad

If you pick up a starving dog and make him prosperous, he will not bite you. This is the principal difference between a dog and a man.

— *Mark Twain*

Choose a job you love, and you will never have to work a day in your life.

— *Confucius*

M ore people rust out than wear out.

— *Dad*

The biggest mistake you can make is to believe that you work for someone else.

— *Unknown*

God gives the nuts, but he does not crack them.

— *Old Proverb*

If you work for a man, in Heaven's name work for him! If he pays you wages that supply your bread and butter, work for him, stand by him, and stand by the institution he represents.

— Elbert Hubbard

Work well done is art.

— Dad

When you can't change the direction of the wind – adjust your sails.

— Dad

You are the same today that you'll be five years from now except for two things: the people you meet and the books you read.

— *Mac McMillan*

People who are resting on their laurels are wearing them on the wrong end.

— *Unknown*

How To Make A Speech:
    Be Sincere
    Be Brief
    Be Seated

— Dad

Art is man's attempt to improve on nature.

— Dad

There are two times in a man's life when he should not speculate: when he can't afford it, and when he can.

— *Mark Twain*

No one ever went broke saving money.

— Dad

To his dog, every man is Napoleon; hence, the constant popularity of dogs.

— Unknown

Each man has a choice in life: he may approach it as a creator or critic, a lover or a hater, a giver or a taker.

— *Unknown*

The greatest ignorance is to reject something you known nothing about.

— *Dad*

Let your policy be quality.

— *Dad*

A diamond is a chunk of coal that made good under pressure.

— *Anonymous*

Laughter has no foreign accent.

— *Paul Lowney*

The man with imagination is never alone.

— Dad

To teach is to learn again.

— *Dad*

Even if you're on the right track, you'll get run over if you just sit there.

— Will Rogers

You never get a second chance to make a good first impression.

— Dad

Life doesn't come with an instruction book —
that's why we have fathers.

— Dad